Edwardian Belfast

The city hall under construction, 28 May 1903. Officially opened in 1906, the new city hall symbolised the prosperity and self-confidence of Edwardian Belfast.

Edwardian Belfast

> We Belfast people are proud of our city and its many activities. We are in the very front of the race of civic development and industrial progress and we have a laudable ambition to keep there and make our mark as it were.[1]

Belfast's 'self-made men in a self-made city'[2] faced the new century with complacency and a profound satisfaction with their own achievements. The inevitability of progress, the miracle of industrial prosperity despite economic decline in rural Ireland suffused the town's Edwardian era. The city's poet wrote of the sweet music of loom and traffic.[3] A visitor believed Belfast should be counted 'amongst the most thrilling industrial centres of Britain'.[4] Already one quarter of the population of Ulster and the eighth city of the United Kingdom, it boasted by 1911 the largest weaving and tobacco factories, ropeworks and output of shipping in the world.[5]

It was a prosperity and satisfaction unequally distributed among its citizens. Class, respectability, income, age, sex and religion divided the Edwardian community and determined one's role and attitude to society. Belfast had many varied images for those who lived within the social enclaves of these barriers.

The hierarchy of class dominated Edwardian society. At its apex were the three hundred families, whose households at Strandtown or on the high ridges of the Antrim and Malone Roads contained a gardener and coachman as well as several indoor servants. Wealth was rarely flaunted. Edwardian Belfast owned at least three millionaires,[6] but it was considered 'uppish' to have male indoor servants. With only one resident blue-blooded aristocrat, Lord Shaftesbury, there was little incentive to emulate the high society which centred round Dublin Castle and its vice-regal courts. Lord Pirrie's lavish entertainments at Ormiston, in a dining room to seat 160 guests, alone strove for more than provincial opulence. They were in many ways a tight-knit group: the men meeting daily for lunch in the Ulster or Reform Clubs and in the board rooms of the town's interlocking companies, or at weekends playing golf together and sailing at Cultra; their wives visiting rarely outside their own circle; their children, educated in English schools, dancing and playing tennis at each others' houses, welding more firmly in their marriages the commercial oligarchy of the town. But they were scarcely isolated from tougher city life. Almost all the men managed personally their own businesses. Their wives sat upon an endless round of committees from Jungle Missions to Nurses for the Sick Poor and, although the gulf was widening with the younger generation, their Roedean daughters continued dutifully to teach in Sunday school.[7]

Much less homogeneous was the central body of the middle classes—a group of five to six thousand families which embraced aspiring barrister and gasworks' clerk. The possession of a maid, the ambition to raise their status, and a fear that that ambition would be thwarted by the demands of that masses bound them loosely together. Buying their suburban houses; cultivating their gardens; educating their children at the fee-paying schools; striving to divert their servants from the superior attractions of

The Ulster Club, Castle Place, 1900.

The Belfast Naturalists' Field Club on an outing to Crebilly House, near Ballymena, 29 June 1907. Organisations such as this, which combined intellectual improvement and fresh air, were well supported by the middle classes.

the mills; saving for their seaside holiday, for sickness and retirement on £200 to £500 a year, they had little sympathy for the rising tide of socialism which would distribute the burdens of the poor and improvident upon their harassed shoulders.

There were fewer social aspirations and financial commitments to burden the skilled artisans, whose 35s. to 45s. wages allowed them to live comfortably in five or six-roomed terrace houses at a 5s. to 6s. rent. Their wives could afford to remain at home while their children attended the national and technical schools. They dug their allotments, attended their lodge or union meeting, or went for a day's trip to Bangor on their trades holiday with only one spectre, a trade recession, on the horizon. And for the majority of Belfast's engineers and shipyard men this remained in the Edwardian period no more than a spectre. They would, however, have claimed that they had earned this comfortable security. They worked a fifty-four hour week. They had served a penurious seven-year apprenticeship to their coveted skilled trade, and they protected that position with a vigorous trade unionism. A labouring élite, which in Britain had reached 'the peak of its pride and position at the end of the nineteenth century, when it represented the undisputed top of the working class world',[8] their scarcity in the unskilled pool of Irish workers enabled them to command wages equal to, or greater than their British fellows. Shipbuilding, engineering and building craftsmen made up 26 per cent of the male, 16 per cent of the total, manual workers of the town.[9] (The labour aristocracy in Britain is estimated to have been 10–15 per cent.[10]) Their concentration and proportion gave them a unity and independence which dominated Belfast's labour. Separated by their economic status from the unskilled labourers they conformed in all, save their trade unionism and manual labour, more closely to the social mores of the white collar workers of the lower middle class. Together they formed the central and largest group of the social hierarchy—the 44 per cent who maintained their station in that final Edwardian classifier, death, by purchasing the £3 plots in the city's graveyards.[11]

But there were 40 per cent who had to be content with the public graves, for the wages of the unskilled were little more than half the craftmen's, and employment more precarious. While agricultural labourers continued to pour into the city, the major construction works which had absorbed the unskilled migrants for forty years shrank markedly in the Edwardian period, and house building had slumped. Even when

The launch of the Titanic, *31 May 1911. The skilled workmen of Belfast's shipyards produced the world's largest liners in this period.*

employment was plentiful there was little security. A cold spell could throw the outdoor labourer out of work, and a strike by the skilled unions, such as the twenty-one week strike of house carpenters in 1900, might leave the unorganised labourer destitute.[12] Few unskilled unions gained many members before 1906, and those which existed had little resources. Only where they worked with skilled tradesmen were they assured of moderate hours. Tram conductors worked a sixty-hour week and carters sixty-eight.

These were the families whose survival depended upon the earnings of the wives or the children. In good times they rented a 3s. 6d. to 4s. 6d. kitchen house as close to work as possible, for trams were a luxury. In bad times they shared a 'double-tenancy' (two upper or ground floor rooms) and their holiday was more often a moonlight flit.[13]

Good and bad times were relative in an existence at subsistence level, but it was only during severe distress that the public conscience was stirred. For the second major division of Belfast's society into those who were, or were not respectable, distorted the Edwardian attitude to the hapless character of poverty. To the middle classes the poor were feckless, dirty, frequently immoral and certainly not respectable. Their dissolute habits and absence of self-help were the causes, not the symptoms of destitution. When the Sandy Row poor received their Christmas treat in 1900 the lord mayor addressed them on 'industry, thrift and honesty, and it was pointed out how these things had made Belfast so prosperous'.[14]

On Sundays Belfast appeared clothed in respectability. Victorian religious observance lingered long in this northern city. Only the occasional tram disturbed the morning congregations, an innovation of which many still disapproved. A proposal to have music in the parks in the afternoons had been more successfully

Belfast washerwoman, c.1905.

Shop assistants—the staff of W. Dobbin & Co., North Street, c.1907.

resisted for it might distract children from Sunday school: but thousands of artisans in their best serge suits crowded around the Custom House steps to hear the methodist choir, the sectarian sermons of the Belfast Protestant Association, or the propaganda of the socialists. Hymns and selections from the oratorios were played in front parlour. In the evening nonconformists might forsake their own congregation to go 'sermon hunting', and in the summer the suburban roads were lined after church with those taking the Sunday walk.

The blanket of sabbatarianism was deceptive. Behind the silence of the main thoroughfares lay areas where church attendance would have caused astonish-

Men sleeping rough in Springfield Brickworks, c.1905. Hogg took this photograph at 3.30 a.m., for the Belfast Central Mission, Grosvenor Hall.

ment,[15] where labourers were sleeping off the effects of a Saturday night of drinking, fighting or wife-beating and where mill women were gossiping or doing the weekly wash. One in fifteen of Ballymacarett's population was estimated to attend church in 1908,[16]

ANDREWS
LIVER
MILKMAID
MILK

The tea bar of the corporation hostel for homeless men, Carrick House, August 1907.

and not all those absent were deterred by the want of decent clothing or the halfpenny for collection. At seven o'clock when the afternoon opening of the public houses ended, the fringes of respectable and unrespectable touched briefly, and church goers hurried past the 'drunken men and women cast out by the publicans just at the very hour all are going to worship God'.[17]

The town's excessive drinking troubled the respectable. 'Saturday night,' said the Rev. Thomas Yates, 'closes on a Belfast soaked in liquor.'[18] Its worst aspect was the methylated spirits still sold in the city, despite the 1880 Spirits Act, for human consumption,[19] but few needed to reach that degradation for whiskey was a penny a tot, and its cheapness blurred the edges of industrial life. Heavy spirit drinking and one licensed house or off-license (generally used by women) for every 328 inhabitants made drunkenness an accepted aspect of the Belfast street. The extent of the problem roused the temperance societies to more vigorous action in the Edwardian era. Even the corporation was persuaded in 1906 to provide municipal temperance posters, and the licensed vintners were driven to complain that Belfast 'had the most agressive so-called temperance party to be found anywhere'.[20] Pledges, bands, demonstrations, banners, and particularly the Catch-My-Pal movement of 1910 slowly took effect, and the Orange parade of that year was considered remarkable 'for the almost entire absence of drunkenness'.[21] The changing attitude to heavy drinking, more than any other factor, drew an increasing proportion of the working classes into the respectable category of the town.

The unrespectable were less easily convinced that their enthusiasm for betting was a certain road to ruin. Although betting shops and street punting were prohibited, and the public libraries blacked out the racing news, bookmakers' touts operated on street corners; the Telly-boys acted as runners; and outwitting the police merely added to the excitement of the gamble.[22] Dog racing came second only to billiards as the evening entertainment of the West Belfast sporting man. Some hired jaunting cars for the Saturday afternoon races at Downpatrick; and the growing interest in watching football was increased by the new football coupons which became popular in the town in 1907. By 1911 a match played by one of the five league teams of the city could draw a crowd of 10,000.[23]

The attempt to curb prostitution was equally well-intentioned but probably misdirected, for the success of the vigilance committee in forcing the police to close the brothels in the centre of the town merely dispersed them into the protesting suburbs.[24] Docks, workhouse and barracks helped to maintain Belfast's reluctant notoriety with Dublin within chaste Ireland. More disturbing, but unquantifiable, was the reputation for reluctant prostitution. The real social evil, in the opinion of a new society, the Irish Council for Public Morals, had its roots in the Irish condemnation of the unmarried mother, and in the low level of female wages, particularly the practice of short-time in the linen industry, which forced single women to exist, at times, on five shillings a week.[25]

In major indictable crime, however, the city's record appears to have been good.[26] The most common, house-breaking, had been checked by the reorganisation and more efficient deployment of the local police between 1904 and 1906, but it rose sharply again in 1912 when the political crisis stretched the resources of the constabulary.[27] The goods displayed outside shop windows and the ease with which they could be converted in the pawnshops added to the most recurrent of the minor cases before the lower courts—petty theft. Pickpockets sometimes came in gangs from England,[28] but were generally local prostitutes and children.

Among the children, magistrates were determined to stamp out a practice which might lead to permanent

crime, and their sentences, against the advice of the prisons' board, were often harsh—three to five years in one of the reformatories, and sometimes shorter terms in prison itself.[29] A more sympathetic and constructive attitude to juvenile offenders had been established by the end of the Edwardian era through the initiative of central government. In 1904 the Irish executive began the experiment of the first United Kingdom separate children's hearings in Belfast and Dublin.[30] The children's act of 1908, which made this children's court statutory, abolished juvenile imprisonment, limited reformatory punishment to those over twelve, and for those convicted under twelve obliged the corporation to assume the maintenance of local industrial schools. Borstal training had been introduced by the Irish prisons' board in 1906. Finally, commital to any institution, save for persistent offenders, declined steadily after 1911 when the probationary system, begun in England in 1907, was extended to the city.[31]

The poor, like the unrespectable, found limited sympathy for having failed to achieve the standards of a city dominated by respectability and success. Belfast did not lack its humanitarians, but individualism and sectarian ethnocentricism retarded the provision, well advanced in British cities by 1914, of a minimum of welfare from the ratepayers' purse. The high death rate, one alderman believed, was due to the careless clothing and tea drinking of the linen workers for the city was 'an elysium for the working classes'.[32] Other councillors thought misery and starvation were 'the fault of the parties themselves', and 'the Corporation was not a eugenic society' to provide for the improvidently begotten large families of labourers.[33] It required the adverse publicity of a royal commission in 1908 to hasten sanitary and health reforms, and

Women prisoners doing laundry work, c.1900. The Ulster Female Pentitentiary was at the corner of Brunswick Street and Franklin Street.

The old clothes and remnant market in 1899.

municipal housing was still-born in the conflict of sectional interests from 1910 to 1914. 'Don't talk to me about the poor labouring classes,' said an estate agent in 1913, 'they are better off than you or I.'[34]

It was difficult for the comfortable to appreciate the economic basis for the widening gulf between them and the poor. Middle-class incomes from investments were flourishing. Education and commercial expansion enabled more 'black-coated workers' to mount the social ladder. Prices, it was true, were rising, but so were wages. Why did the poor seem poorer?

Wages, in fact, increased more slowly and erratically than prices. While the municipal labourers' wage—one of the highest and most amenable to pressure in the city—rose from 19s. to 21s. 6d. in the Edwardian

Belfast market woman, c.1905.

period,[35] the sovereign of 1895 could buy only 16s. 3d. worth of food by 1912.[36] And food was the largest item in the household budget of the poor. In 1909 the Belfast board of guardians estimated that the minimum subsistence income for a family with three children was 22s. 5d.: food 12s. 8d.; rent 3s. 6d.; clothing 2s. 3d.; fuel and light 2s.; household and cleaning materials 1s.; and 1s. for luxuries such as tram fares, newspapers and tobacco.[37]

Economies were made by reducing the variety and quality of food. Tea, white bread, sugar and condensed milk were the staple of the Belfast labouring class.[38] Health visitors deplored the fact that the town's working wives had abandoned the country tradition of porridge, wheaten bread and potatoes,[39] but many

KELVIN
THE KELVIN PICT
& MILLINERY
WAREROOMS

Kelvin Picture Palace, 17–18 College Square East, in 1911 or 1912. The cinema took its name from the famous scientist, Lord Kelvin, who was born there in 1818.

lacked time, fuel or the facilities for cooking on the open kitchen fires.[40] Three quarters of the kitchen houses surveyed in 1901 did not use gas.[41] It was not until the introduction of coin meters in 1903 removed the bogey of the long-term bill, that gas lamps and, more slowly, cooking rings, began to appear in the poorer homes.[42] Margarine, American bacon and cheap foreign meat, sold from barrows, relieved the monotonous diet.[43] Many of the thrifty still kept a pig in the backyard, although these were more firmly forbidden when detected after 1905.[44] Periwinkles for boiling and mussels and cockles, eaten raw, were bought until 1908 from the hawkers' carts which toured in the evenings the working-class streets—a primary source, it was believed, of the high typhoid incidence in the city.[45] Their proscription encouraged the spread of a new gastronomic luxury, the Italian ice-cream, fish and chip shop, which entered Belfast at the turn of the century. By 1914 there were forty-nine,[46] their gay colours, bright lights, gramophone music and hot food supplying a counter rivalry to the older neighbourhood focus of the pub.

Gaiety flecked the drabness of Belfast's poverty. Robert Lynd, who was no great admirer of his native city, admitted that its people had a 'promising gladness'.[47] The spinning rooms resounded to the singing of Connolly's 'linen slaves', and the mill girls answered Countess Markiewicz' impassioned plea for cultural activities by happily pelting her with snowballs.[48] This was a city of bands and ballads, a folk culture which absorbed hymns, music hall songs, Irish airs and the faded repertoire of the Italian organ grinders into a music of its own.

> There weren't any films in those days to help us learn the ways of the outside world, we lived our own lives dancing the night through and singing our songs . . .[49]

It was a gaiety which depended upon the intimacy of neighbourhoods which shared the same pleasures and privations. The wakes of the Pound, the short-time which anguished the Bone, the 'white-work' which filled the kitchens of Sandy Row,[50] drew communities together. When the films did come—fifteen picture houses by 1914—they, too, drew their regular patrons from the same familiar neighbourhood.

It was, therefore, to their own community that the poor turned when illness or unemployment upset the family budget. '. . . it was your friends and neighbours who helped you until you were lucky to get work.'[51] The pawnshop was the next remedy. Clothing, bought on the cheque or ticket system, or second-hand from the Smithfield shops and church missions, was an investment of capital, readily convertible. Pawnbrokers charged up to fivepence in the pound on loans repaid within one month, and their expansion from 100 in 1900 to 117 in 1914 is an indication of their importance in the Edwardian economy of the poor. Many of their patrons were habituated to the twice-weekly journey, but the more respectable were sensitive about using them and employed pawnbrokers' runners. The moneylender, usually a woman living in the street, was the last resource for she charged 15 per cent. Charity, distributed mainly by clergymen, could be generous, but depended often upon church membership, and only the orphan money was thought compatible with self-respect.[52]

State charity with its stigma of pauperism was to be avoided at all costs. The dread of going 'up the Lisburn Road'[53] hung over the poor, who preferred to send their children temporarily onto the streets rather than be separated from them in the union.[54] In consequence only 3 to 4 per cent of the workhouse inmates were able-bodied paupers,[55] and the device of publicly displaying in their districts the names of those receiving out-relief[56] helped to maintain in Belfast the lowest pauper rate in the United Kingdom. To the credit of the guardians it was a primacy in which they took little pride, for it stemmed from the insistence of the Irish

local government board that it was no part of the guardians' duty to alleviate poverty, and that out-relief must be curtailed since it demoralised the recipients.[57] Their vigilance ensured that, although the numbers granted out-relief rose from 238 in 1901 to 888 in 1914, this was still far below comparable British cities. Bristol, for example, gave aid to more than four thousand outside its workhouse; Glasgow eighteen thousand.[58]

But Westminster had outstipped the Irish executive and the individualist city in recognising that poverty might require more positive state alleviation. For some of its causes, especially unemployment, sickness and old age, Edwardian social legislation assumed public responsibility. In the depression of 1908–9 a grant under the unemployed workmen act of 1905 enabled the municipal distress committee to provide work for 3,227 men, some three quarters of the applicants. In 1910 its functions were taken over by the first local labour exchange.[59] A year later part II of the National Insurance Act, applied experimentally at first to the shipbuilding, engineering and building trades, secured in Belfast a considerable section of the town's male labour force against temporary unemployment by compulsory contributions and a benefit of seven shillings a week. The health insurance provisions of part I of the act went further. *All* manual workers who earned less than £160 a year qualified for sickness benefit by joining an approved society and paying fourpence, or for women threepence a week, although the continuation in Ireland of the old dispensary ticket system delayed what might have been a greater reform in preventive medicine among the town's industrial workers.[60] The most direct and immediate relief for poverty came from the five-shilling old-age pension. In 1909 three quarters of the town's population over

Male paupers at the Belfast union workhouse, Lisburn Road, c.1903.

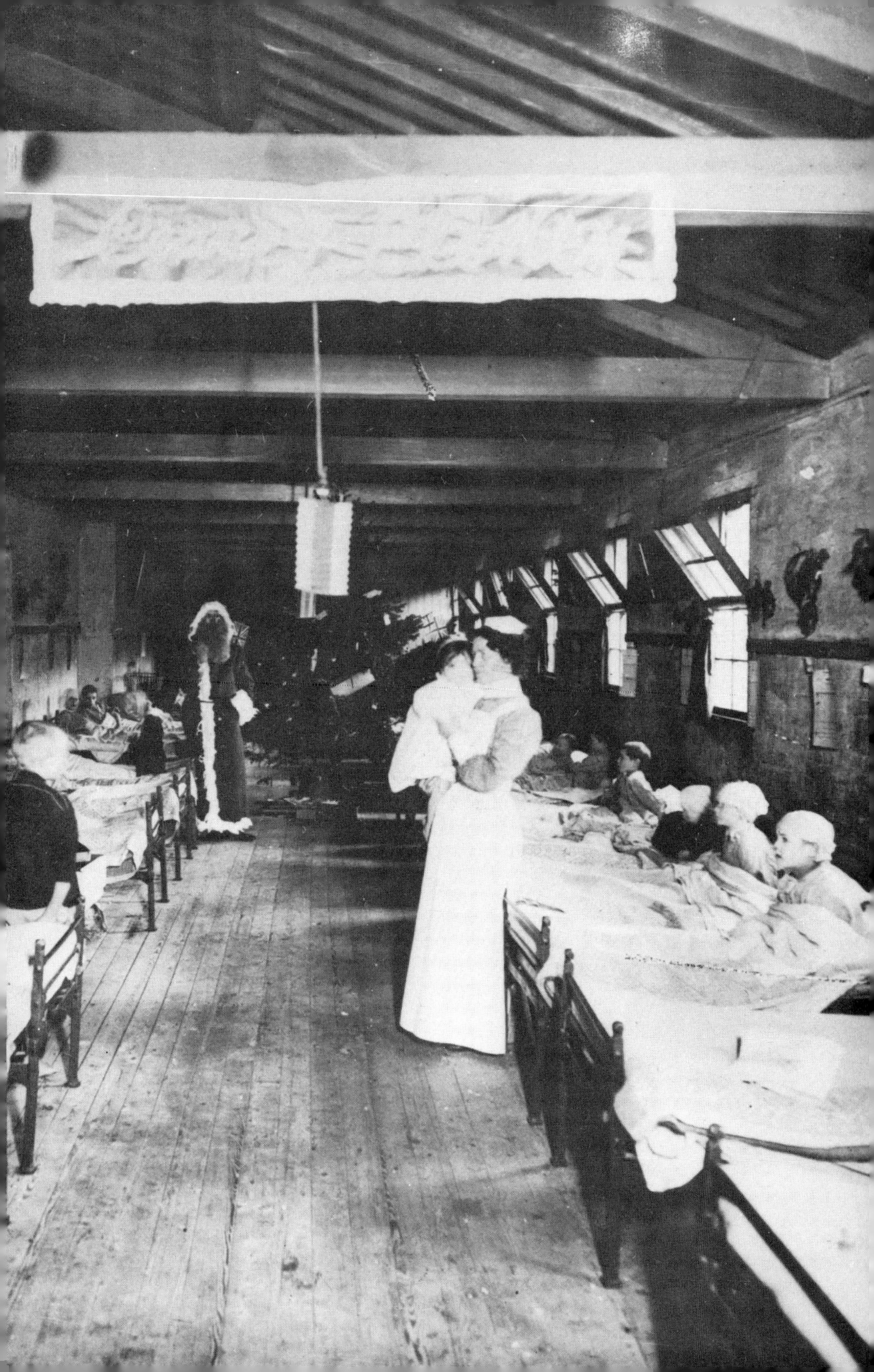

seventy, some seven thousand who had an income under ten shillings a week, qualified for the new grant.[61] The dread of the poor, the pauperism of old age, had at last been removed.

At the other end of Belfast's age division, however, much was said and less achieved in mitigating the social inequalities among the city's children. Those who came within the care of the workhouse were perhaps the more fortunate, for a boarding-out committee, formed in 1900,[62] helped to transfer the majority to foster homes, arranged apprenticeships, assisted emigration and followed their careers with anxiety and pride. But these were only a fraction of the child victims of society. As in Dublin child beggars abounded, encouraged rather than dissuaded by the 1903 by-laws which licensed children for street trading. Others fully earned their income. Some hawked sticks; fifty or sixty girls sold flowers; another fifty girls carried messages; 450 were errand boys; and three quarters of the thousand newsboys were of school age, coming onto the streets at three o'clock to earn six or seven shillings a week. Ragged, barefooted, 'regular sharpers' and addicted to pitch and toss, many drifted from the sheltering care of the city missions to the independence of the North Street lodging houses, and many eventually entered reformatories or became loafers.[63] Finally there were the two to three thousand half-timers, aged from twelve to fourteen, who alternated days at school and in the linen mills to earn three to four shillings a week. Easily recognisable, their teachers said, from their sallow complexions and unchildlike demeanour, few reached the fifth standard, for the adult day in the hot mill atmosphere left them little energy or enthusiasm for book-learning.[64]

They were not the only children whose education in

A children's ward in the union infirmary, Christmas 1909 or 1910. The children's hospital was opened in the summer of 1909.

Abbey Street from Peter's Hill, 26 April 1912. Hogg took a number of similar photographs of slum housing condemned under the Belfast Improvement Order of 1910. The bulk of housing in Belfast was constructed in the later part of the nineteenth century when building regulations existed to impose certain standards, and so the city compared favourably with other industrial centres in regard to its standard of housing. Little was done, however, until 1910 to remove slum dwellings built before the passing of these regulations.

Edwardian Belfast fell shamefully below the national standard. The church schools had neither the accommodation, nor were they effectively dispersed to absorb the soaring numbers of the town's protestant children. Where the need was greatest in the newer industrial districts congregations were non-existent or too poor to provide building extensions. Fifteen thousand Belfast children were without school places.[65] One third of the schools had no playgrounds; in 1914 fifty-five were considered constantly overcrowded.[66] Classes jostled each other in the single large schoolroom, were packed out of the way onto the steps of the wooden gallery, or overflowed into corridors and cloakrooms.[67] Little wonder there was no inducement to improve the low rate of attendance among those on the rolls (5 to 15 per cent below England and Scotland[68]). In 1912 seventeen thousand were estimated to be absent every day,[69] and a generation of Ballymacarett's children found their education on the streets.[70]

They can scarcely be said to have felt the deprivation. The streets were the playgrounds of the Belfast children and they made them their own. Skipping, roller skating, hop scotch, tig and piggy, footballs, go-carts, peries and swings from lamp-posts imperilled the by-passer. There were policemen to be taunted and corner boys to provoke. There were travelling penny shows[71] and Germans with dancing bears.[72] Twopence would buy a seat in the Empire to hear Harry Lauder or Marie Lloyd, and the penniless could resell the programmes of the first house and sit in unwashed splendour in the first row of the Hippodrome gallery.[73] A bottle of water and 'a piece' sustained one on longer excursions, bluebell-picking up the Lagan tow path, netting spricklies in the Bog Meadows, gathering cockles on the lough shore. There were May Queens and Hallowe'en to go a' begging, bands to follow every evening, bonfires to celebrate one's politics, and one's religion to demonstrate on the Sunday-school trip.

York Road National School, c.1910, at an entrance of York Street Spinning Mill. Some of the pupils at this school would have been half-timers.

Between the national and grammar school children there remained a deep gulf. The social revolution set in motion in England by the scholarships of 1902 did not touch the city. One in eighteen primary children passed into secondary education in Great Britain,[74] compared with one in sixty of Belfast's national schoolboys,[75] for the grammar schools offered few open scholarships and their curriculum had little practical value as commercial or technical training.

One significant transformation occurred in middle-class education. In 1900 neither co-education nor Mrs Byers' formidable success in Victoria had convinced some parents that their daughters should share the expense or rigours of public examinations. The city contained fifty-five schools for 'young ladies',[76] the majority offering, sometimes to a mere handful of pupils, a second-rate education by unqualified teachers or continental governesses in ill-converted private houses.[77] Unwilling to admit state inspectors after 1902 and presenting few pupils for the state examinations barely a dozen qualified for an education grant. By 1914 most had succumbed. A few, employing the new generation of women graduates, recognising the day school market and transferring to boards of governors, became the twentieth-century Belfast girls' schools. Some of the personal touch was lost. Proprietors like Miss Hunter at Princess Gardens would no longer plait the girls' hair or administer cough mixture,[78] but girls had entered a tougher intellectual discipline.

The masculine preserves were shrinking elsewhere in the Edwardian city. This was the age of the 'new woman', a minority of an educated and leisured middle class who subjected local society to a critical and feminine reappraisal. They investigated, spoke and wrote on alcoholism, crime, child cruelty, primary education, 'sweating', infant mortality and venereal disease. They raised funds and set up pioneering clinics and shelters; but their ability to influence public policy directly was negligible. Although women, as elected poor law guardians after 1898, brought a practical reorganisation to the administration of the workhouse, they were ineligible as municipal candidates until 1911, and without the parliamentary franchise, politicians could afford to neglect their opinion. Inevitably, therefore, these middle-class reformers were the core of the city's suffrage movement.[79]

The most active of the local groups was the Irish Women's Suffrage Society. Infected with an evangelical crusading spirit they met weekly from 1908, organised open-air meetings, chalked pavements, paraded with

Platform party at a meeting of women Unionists in the Ulster Hall, c.1905.

posters and toured the provincial towns.[80] For the unionist women who were rolling bandages, learning semaphore and copying the male organisations of the political crisis they had nothing but scorn. They were not 'door mats' and would dare to challenge even Carson by shouting 'Votes for women' through a megaphone as the covenant parade passed their office in Donegall Place.[81]

But it was the unionist women's tactics which proved effective. In September 1913 British and Dublin suffragists were astounded to hear the Ulster provisional government would be based on the municipal franchise, which included middle-class women, and would co-opt women onto its committees. Ulster suffragists were jubilant that their province would be second in Europe to admit women to political participation (Norway was first in 1913). Carson, however, began to hedge upon the extension of the municipal franchise beyond the initial referendum.[83] Thereupon the envoys of the militant British Women's Social and Political Union, who had arrived in the city in 1912, declared war. Their campaign of treacle and paint in pillar boxes, slogans carved on golf greens, arson and even assaults upon the hostile editors of the *Belfast Telegraph* and *News Letter* ended only with the wartime amnesty. To the majority of local suffragists the militancy was superfluous and embarassing. They had gained their first victory and were content to wait.[85]

A more significant advance in female emancipation had been taking place less dramatically. Single women were acquiring a greater security and independence in increasing opportunities for employment and in better wages and conditions at work. Exploitation of cheap female labour contracted. Between 1901 and 1911 the number of maids in the city fell by one thousand. Milliners and dressmakers also suffered, for ready-made clothing reduced the sweated workshops of the department stores. Shop assistants were still grossly underpaid and sternly disciplined, and they worked at least until 8 p.m. on weekdays and 10.30 on Saturdays; but the living-in system was declining, and the shops act of 1911 ensured that all had a half-holiday.[86] Wages and hours, however, were regulated in the expanding making-up factories by the trade boards act of 1909,

Workers in Belfast worsted wool factory, c.1915.

and in the shirt factories in 1913, so that these ware-room girls became the cynosure of local female labour, and piece work enabled a skilled stitcher to earn 14s. to 24s. a week.[87] Training courses in the new Royal and the reorganised City hospitals raised the status and attraction of nursing. There were 154 nurses in 1901 and 653 by 1911. Typists invaded the business offices:

one thousand female clerks in 1901 became two thousand a decade later.[88]

The result was a new phenomenon in Belfast society—the teenage flapper. With screw curls falling from halo hats, uniform blouses and abbreviated skirts boldly displaying their ankles, irrepressible giggles, catch-phrases and knowing winks, they crowded the business-men's trams and thronged Royal Avenue in the evening.[89] In their work and women's magazines they had glimpsed a middle-class luxury and domestic emancipation they were determined to acquire: carpet-sweepers, vacuum-cleaners, gas stoves and electric lighting. By 1914 they had realised that birth control would bring this world within their reach.[90] Women's concept of her role in society had changed fundamentally.

In one respect the balance of Belfast society did not change, although the Edwardian community was shaken deeply by the attempts to readjust it. Catholics had failed to gain more than a subordinate place in the socio-economic and political hierarchy of Ulster's capital. In 1901, although they were half the population of the province they were only 23.4 per cent of the city, and protestant capital and enterprise continued to dominate Belfast. Fear of a catholic engulfment, trade-union hostility to cheap catholic labour, unionist suspicion that Irish nationalism would undermine Belfast's prosperity, and perhaps the vicious circle of initial poverty, narrowed effectively the roads to catholic advancement. They were, for example, 32 per cent of the general labourers but only 7 per cent of the skilled shipyard workers, 13 per cent of the clerks and 12 per cent of the managers and manufacturers.[91]

At the turn of the century a new confidence reinvigorated the catholic community. Supported by a reviving sense of Irish identity and Gaelic culture and by the growing influence of the Irish party at Dublin Castle and Westminster, a Catholic Association had

Class in design room, School of Art, May 1907.

been formed under the guidance of the bishop of Down and Connor, the Most Rev. Dr Henry Henry, to assert the catholic claim to political expression and social opportunity within the town. Its immediate success in forcing the corporation to concede two catholic wards within the extended city of 1896 encouraged the new councillors and the association to press on with agitation for a proportionate catholic share in public employment. At the same time the protestant and unionist monopoly of demonstrations was challenged. The march to Hannahstown, which had provoked the 1872 riots, was defiantly revived in 1896, '98 and '99.[92] In 1901 the first catholic religious procession for fifty years was held in the city.[93] In 1903 a torchlight parade of 12,000 welcomed Joseph Devlin's return to West

Belfast.[94] The challenge was not ignored. Support for a counter movement, the Belfast Protestant Association, soared. Sectarian propaganda, fear and animosity permeated the opening years of the Edwardian city.[95] Parades were attacked. Rioting again became endemic,[96] and the police admitted that they dared not enter the shipyards to prevent the assaults there.[97]

The violence shocked the participants and the authorities into responsibility.[98] Between 1903 and 1908 Belfast seemed to be approaching a reconcilement of its communities. The Belfast Protestant Association shrank into insignificance, sobered by the imprisonment of three of its leaders in 1901, and puzzled by the liberalizing speeches of its M.P., Thomas Sloan.[99] The Catholic Association, too, was losing support. Redmond would not recognise it, for the Irish cause, he had reminded its members, was not just a catholic cause.[100] In 1905 it was forced to dissolve, and Devlin, who had deplored its union of religion and politics, won West Belfast in 1906. It was, he declared after his election, a moment for catholic and protestant at last to meet and shake hands across the Boyne.[101]

But external politics would not allow Belfast's citizens to come to terms. To 'Home Rule' or the 'Union' they were committed, and in that gathering storm Belfast's bridge-building disintegrated. Sectarian animosity reflamed. The Twelfth in 1909 was accompanied by three nights of serious rioting between Nationalists and police.[102] The year 1910 ended with protestant and catholic clergy, congregations and politicians incensed beyond compassion by their conflicting attitudes to the mixed marriages of the *Ne Temere* decree.[103] By November 1911 ten thousand were attending the B.P.A.'s meeting at the Customs' House steps.[104] In the summer of 1912 two thousand catholics were driven temporarily from the shipyards, three hundred permanently from the city.[105] Bonfires in the Pound celebrated the third reading of the home rule bill, but the clergy patrolled its streets.[106] In the spring of 1914, while 24,000 Ulster volunteers waited in the city to resist the coming act, Belfast's Irish volunteers trained for defence seven miles beyond the Falls. Three thousand men and sixty nurses and doctors waited apprehensively for the attack they believed would come.[107]

Instead the Great War and the creation of the Northern Ireland state separate the Edwardian city from contemporary Belfast. The cold winds of post-war depression pierced the family firms and chilled the drawing rooms of Ireland's linenopolis. The curfew descended upon the bloodshed of the Troubles. Catholics retired from constructive political opposition to the smouldering resentment of the ghetto. In the thirties wooden barriers were erected to keep the warring factions apart. The skilled shipyard men's pride crumbled in the dole queues. But there *was* a dole, and labourers and women, catholic as well as protestant, joined them in the queue. Municipal schools were built on some of the gardens of the villas, and each year fifty city scholars, girls as well as boys, won free places in the grammar schools. Two women sat on the city council. Two hundred and fifty corporation houses stood amid the growing slums of West Belfast. It was not the urban future its Edwardian citizens had envisaged, but the fulcrum of advantage had been marginally displaced.

Notes

ABBREVIATIONS

N.L.I.	National Library of Ireland
P.R.O.	Public Record Office (London)
P.R.O.N.I.	Public Record Office of Northern Ireland (Belfast)
S.P.O.	State Paper Office

1. *Belfast News Letter,* 12 Sept. 1899.
2. Ibid., 26 Mar. 1900.
3. Richard Rowley, 'To a poet' in *City songs and others* (Dublin, 1918), pp 16–17.
4. Louis Paul-Dubois, *Contemporary Ireland* (Dublin, 1908), p. 102.
5. *Weekly Irish Times,* 19 Aug. 1911.
6. Wealth is difficult to assess after Harcourt's death duties of 1894. Gifts made more than a year before death (3 years after 1909) were not included in probate, and the practice of such gifts grew. Despite this, two of Belfast's distillers left £1 m. each in the Edwardian era and a third partner was reputed to be richer. Lord Pirrie was rumoured to be a multi-millionaire. Fortunes were made more easily before the graduated income tax of 1909. At that date at least three of Belfast's citizens were said to pay tax on incomes over £30,000 p.a., in contrast to 1957 when there was no taxed income in Northern Ireland over £20,000 p.a. *Nomad's Weekly,* 8 May 1909, and K. S. Isles and Norman Cuthbert, *An economic survey of Northern Ireland* (Belfast, 1957), p. 16.

7. I am indebted to Commander P. Smiles, O.B.E., for his graphic recollections of this society.
8. E. J. Hobsbawm, *Industry and empire,* (London, 1968), p. 247, quoted in P. Thompson, 'Memory and history', in *Social Science Research Council Newsletter,* no. 6 (June 1969), p. 18.
9. *Census of Ireland, 1911, province of Ulster, city of Belfast,* 12 [C 6051-I], H.C. 1912-13, cxvi, 1.
10. Thompson, op. cit., p. 18.
11. Between 1901 and 1914 in the two municipal cemeteries 1.2 per cent purchased £10 plots; 15 per cent £4; 43.8 per cent £3 or under; and 40 per cent paid the 2s. 6d. interment fee for the public plots (Belfast corporation, burial class fund, *Abstract of accounts 1901-14*). The gradations, although a useful social indicator, have an upward bias for they do not include the private cemetery for catholics, whose occupational status is clearly lower than the nonconformists in the census returns.
12. Minutes of the Belfast and District Trades and Labour Council, 1898-1901, 21 Sept. 1900.
13. Local government board inquiry, no. 39., improvement scheme, 1911 (City Hall, Belfast).
14. *Belfast News Letter,* 5 Jan. 1900.
15. *Nomad's Weekly,* 14 Apr. 1906.
16. Ibid., 25 July 1908. This was considerably below the 20 per cent for Camberwell in 1902-3 or Middlesborough's 23 per cent in 1906 (H. J. Dyos, *Victorian suburb* (Leicester, 1961), pp 157-8, and Lady F. E. E. Bell, *At the works* (London, 1907), p. 10). Belfast had no comparable general census, but attendance in the suburbs and in the catholic districts would have been much higher than in Ballymacarett, where the churches had failed to keep pace with its expansion between 1860 and 1900.
17. *Belfast Telegraph,* 26 Oct. 1898.
18. Ibid., 5 Oct. 1898.
19. *Nomad's Weekly,* 14 June, 1913.
20. *Belfast Telegraph,* 17 Apr. 1906.
21. Inspector general's and county inspectors' reports, 1910 (P.R.O., C.O. 904/81).
22. *Northern Whig,* 4-11 Oct. 1905. *Report of the inter-departmental committee of the employment of*

children, especially in street trading, in the large centres of population in Ireland, with evidence and appendices, 110 [C 1144], H.C. 1902, xlix, 334. This report is hereafter cited as *Street Trading.*

23. *Nomad's Weekly,* 28 Jan. 1911.
24. Ibid., 14 June, 1913.
25. *Belfast Telegraph,* 24 Apr. 1913.
26. Intelligence notes 1914, p. 5 (S.P.O.).
27. S.P.O., C.S.O., R.P. 6781/1904. Intelligence notes 1912–13 (P.R.O., C.O. 903/17).
28. Minutes of the tramway and electricity committee, 1906, f. 125 (Belfast corporation transport department).
29. Convictions and depositions, petty sessions, Belfast 1900 (P.R.O.N.I., CLX.iv/9).
30. *Twenty-eighth report of the general prisons board of Ireland, 1905–6,* viii, 44 and 45 [C 3103], H.C. 1906, 52, 108 and 109.
31. Margaret Kinnaird, 'A survey of child welfare in Belfast' (unpublished M.A. thesis, Queen's University, Belfast, 1924) (hereafter cited as Kinnaird, *Child welfare*), p. 31.
32. *Belfast News Letter,* 5 Mar. 1896.
33. *Northern Whig,* 7 May 1913.
34. Local government board inquiry, 4–5 Dec. 1913, p. 162 (City Hall, Belfast).
35. *Northern Whig,* 2 Apr. 1913.
36. *Belfast News Letter,* 9 May, 1913.
37. *The Irish Nation,* 20 Feb. 1909.
38. H. W. Bailie, *Report of the medical superintendent officer of health, 1910* (Belfast, 1911), p. 84. *Report of the departmental committee on humidity and ventilation in flax mills and linen factories: evidence,* p. 89 [C 7466] H.C. 1914, xxxvi, 199.
39. Special reports, no. 2. 1903–12, f. 115, p. 8 (City Hall, Belfast).
40. A. Fennell, *Letters on primary education* (Belfast, 1905), 16 Jan. 1904.
41. Special reports, no. 1, 1898–1904, ff 114–5 (City Hall, Belfast).
42. Ibid., f. 206.
43. *Nomad's Weekly,* 28 Aug. 1913.
44. H. W. Bailie, *Report of the medical superintendent of health, 1906* (Belfast, 1907), p. 32.

45. *Belfast health commission: report to the local government board for Ireland,* 28 and 132–3 [C 4128], H.C., 1908, xxxi, 734 and 860–1.
46. *Belfast Directory, 1900, 1914.*
47. Robert Lynd, *Home life in Ireland,* (London, 1909), p. 186.
48. Ellen Grimley MS, pp 22–3 (N.L.I., MS 13,096).
49. Ibid., p. 13.
50. *Street trading,* pp 146–7, 370–1.
51. R. H. McIlborough's notebooks (P.R.O.N.I., D.O.D. 770).
52. Kinnaird, *Child welfare,* p. 44.
53. *Belfast Telegraph,* 17 Aug. 1910.
54. *Street trading,* p. 102, 326.
55. Minutes of the Belfast board of guardians 1914, p. 33 (P.R.O.N.I., BG vii/A/93).
56. Ibid., 1908, p. 737 (P.R.O.N.I., BG vii/A/81).
57. Ibid., 1911, p. 199 (P.R.O.N.I., BG vii/A/87).
58. *Labour Gazette, 1901–14* (P.R.O.N.I., D. 2088/2/5).
59. Minutes of the distress committee, 13 Oct. 1908–7 Jan. 1910 (City Hall, Belfast).
60. *Irish Citizen,* 24 Jan. 1914.
61. Special reports, no. 2, 1903–12, f. 106 (City Hall, Belfast).
62. Minutes of the Belfast board of guardians 1899–1900, p. 688 (P.R.O.N.I., BG vii/A/65).
63. *Street trading,* pp vi, 67–98, 214, 291–322.
64. Ibid., pp x, 82–7, 113, 218, 306–11, 337. *Hansard 4,* clxxxiv, 19 Feb. 1908, 811. *78th report of the commissioners of national education in Ireland, part I,* 101–4 [C 7061], H.C. 1914, xxvii, 423–6.
65. *Hansard 5,* lxi, 16 Apr. 1914, 402.
66. H. W. Bailie, *Report of the medical superintendent of health, 1914* (Belfast, 1915), p. 98.
67. *72nd report of the commissioners of national education in Ireland, part I,* 146–52 [C 3185], H.C., 1906, xxix, 894–900.
68. *First report of the vice-regal committee of enquiry into education in Ireland, part I,* 125 [C 6829], H.C. 1913, xxii, 235. This report is hereafter cited as *Vice-regal enquiry.*
69. *78th report of the commissioners of national education in Ireland, part I,* p. 102, 424.

70. *Vice-regal enquiry,* p. 125.
71. Minutes of the Belfast board of guardians, 1914, p. 271 (P.R.O.N.I., BG vii/A/93).
72. *Nomad's Weekly,* 7 July 1906.
73. Ibid., 2 Feb. 1907.
74. William Ashworth, *An economic history of England 1870–1939* (London, 1960), p. 197.
75. *Vice-regal enquiry,* pp 114–5.
76. *Belfast directory 1900,* p. 85.
77. *Report on primary education in Ireland,* 26, 40–42 [C 1981], H.C., 1904, xx, 976, 990–92.
78. *The lamp: Princess Gardens School 1865–1965* (Belfast, 1965), p. 12.
79. The first suffrage society in the city was formed in 1870 by Isabella Todd, a leading speaker in the unionist campaigns against Home rule in 1885-6 and 1892. Its success in wooing the support of unionist leaders obtained the extension to Belfast of the British middle-class women's municipal franchise of 1869 in the city's local franchise act of 1887—eleven years before this was conceded to Ireland as a whole.
    A second source of Belfast's 'new women' came from the graduates of the Royal University. Queen's College admitted women in 1881, and, after the medical course had been opened to women in 1891, they were the first in Europe to share male dissecting rooms. Belfast's women doctors, particularly Drs Elizabeth Bell and Marion Andrews, were to play a notable part in the local twentieth-century suffrage movement and in creation of mother and child welfare services in the city.
    In the mounting United Kingdom campaign for the parliamentary franchise from 1907 the older Belfast societies continued to concentrate on winning privately the individual support of unionist leaders, of whom the most influential convert was James Craig. A new local society, the Irish Women's Suffrage Society, avoided political allegiance and used greater publicity to gain the attention of the general male voters.
80. *Irish Citizen,* 7 Sept. 1912.
81. Ibid., 26 Oct. 1912.
82. Ibid., 20 and 27 Sept. 1913.
83. Ibid., 14 Mar. 1914.

84. Judicial proceedings 1911–17 (P.R.O., C.O. 904/32).
85. *Irish Citizen,* 13 June 1914.
86. *Belfast Health Journal,* Feb. 1905. *Nomad's Weekly,* 6 Aug. 1912.
87. *Conditions of employment in the linen and other making-up trades of the north of Ireland,* 92 [C 6509], H.C., 1912–13, xxxiv, 484.
88. *Census of Ireland, 1901, province of Ulster, city of Belfast,* [C 1123a], H.C. 1902, cxxvi, I.
89. *Nomad's Weekly,* 14 Sept. 1907.
90. *Anon., Infantile mortality* (Belfast, 1906), pp 1 and 22. Industrial migration produced a youthful population (77 per cent under forty in 1901) and a high marriage rate (8.2 per 1000 against Ireland's 4.8 in 1891–1901), which contributed to Belfast's high birth rate (30.4 per 1000 against Ireland's 23.1 between 1901 and 1911). Restricted families show first in the middle class dispensary returns (College district, 20.1 in 1914) but were still high in both protestant and catholic working class districts. Belfast's fertility decrease in the decade before 1902 had been the second lowest in European major cities, but in the Edwardian era there was an increasing public deprecation of the Malthusian effects of the large families of the labourers. (*Census, 1901 and 1911.* Birth rates for dispensary districts in the annual *Reports of the medical superintendents of health,* (Belfast, 1900–1914). Sir C. A. Cameron, *Report upon the state of the public health in the city of Dublin for the year 1914* (Dublin, 1915), p. 33. *Nomad's Weekly,* 18 Nov. 1905. *Belfast Telegraph,* 19 Apr. 1907).
91. *Census of Ireland, Belfast,* 1901, 15–25, 203–13.
92. S.P.O., C.S.O.R.P. 11935/1912 and 15358/1900.

Ibid., 1388/1901 and 11764/1901.

94. Ibid., 12312/1903.
95. Ibid., 16363/1907. *Belfast Telegraph,* 18 June 1901.
96. S.P.O., C.S.O.R.P. 11935/1912.
97. Ibid., 12385/1901.
98. Ibid., 13517/1901.
99. Inspector general's and county inspectors' reports 1906–8 (S.P.O., Crime Branch Special 937/S, 1949/S, 2079/S.
100. *Irish News,* 15 Sept. 1900.
101. Ibid., 10 Feb. 1906.

102. Intelligence notes 1909, p. 64 (P.R.O., C.O. 903/15).
103. Ibid., 1910, pp 44–6 (P.R.O., C.O. 903/16). *Belfast Telegraph,* 11 Jan. 1911.
104. Inspector general's and county inspectors' reports, 1911 (P.R.O., C.O. 904/85).
105. S.P.O., C.S.O.R.P. 15601/1912.
106. Inspector general's and county inspectors' reports, 1913 (P.R.O., C.O. 904/89).
107. Berkley MS (N.L.I., MS 7880).

An earlier draft of the text appeared in the Belfast Telegraph, *1 Sept. 1970.*

Acknowledgements

Grateful acknowledgement is made to the Ulster Museum for its co-operation, and for permission to reproduce nineteen photographs from its Hogg Collection. The photographs on pages 46 and 48 are reproduced by kind permission of the Public Record Office of Northern Ireland and the Belfast College of Technology. Thanks are also due to the Department of Education (Northern Ireland) for their generous grant towards publication of this book.

Overleaf:

Laying electric tramway rails, looking down York Street from the junction of Donegall Street and Royal Avenue, 1905. Improvement of Belfast transport facilities in the late nineteenth and early twentieth centuries was essential for the growth of the city, allowing people to travel considerable distances to their place of work.

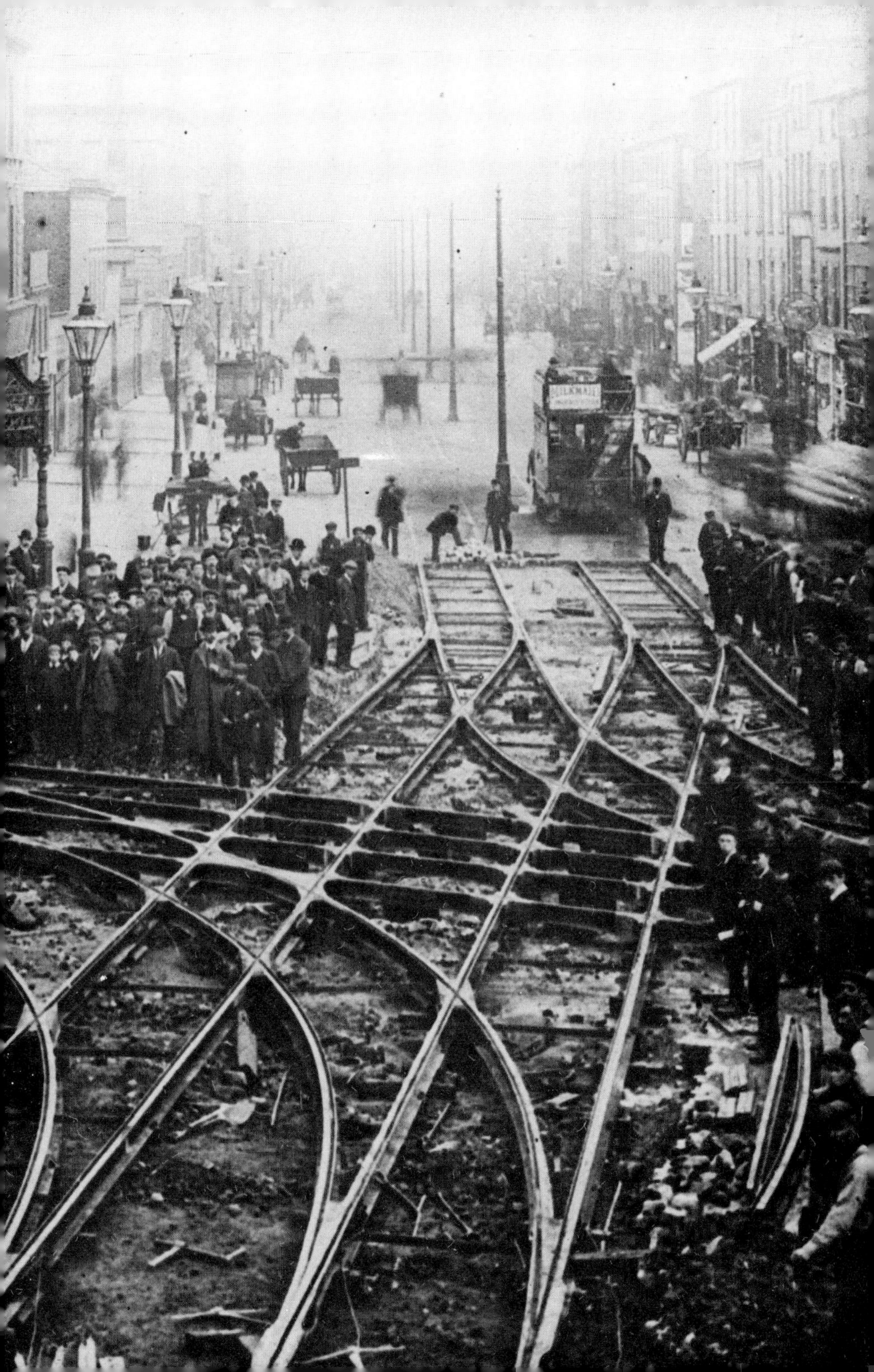